# CHAMPION CRACK-UPS

## MORE THAN 150 SENSATIONAL SPORTS JOKES

**KINGFISHER**

First published 2008 by Kingfisher
an imprint of Macmillan Children's Books
a division of Macmillan Publishers Limited
20 New Wharf Road, London N1 9RR
Basingstoke and Oxford
Associated companies throughout the world
www.panmacmillan.com

ISBN: 978-0-7534-1585-6

3 5 7 9 8 6 4

A CIP catalogue record for this book is available from the British Library.

Printed in India
3TR/THOM/PICA/80STORA/C

# CHAMPION CRACK-UPS

## MORE THAN 150 SENSATIONAL SPORTS JOKES

Illustrated by Gary Swift

KINGFISHER

**How do you start
a jelly race?**
*Say, "Get set."*

**What's a vampire's
favourite sport?**
*Skin diving.*

**What happens when a
sailing boat gets old?**
*It keels over.*

**Who won the milk drinking contest?**
*The cat. It lapped the field.*

**Why did the potato go to the match?**
*So it could root for the home team.*

**What kind of child can jump higher than a house?**
*All kinds. Houses can't jump!*

# WHO NEEDS BRAINS?

A coach walked into the locker room before a game, looked over to his star player and said, "I'm not supposed to let you play since you failed maths, but we need you in there. So, I'm going to ask you a maths question, and if you get it right, you can play."

The player agreed, so the coach looked into his eyes intently and asked, "Okay, now concentrate hard and tell me the answer to this: What is two plus two?"

The player thought for a moment and then answered, "Four?"

"Did you say four?" the coach exclaimed, excited that he had got it right.

Suddenly, all the other players on the team began screaming . . .

"Come on Coach, give him another chance!"

A tap, a lettuce and a tomato were having a race . . . what happened?
*The tap was running, the lettuce was ahead, and the tomato was trying to ketchup.*

What did the bumblebee striker say?
*"Hive scored!"*

Susie: I went riding at the weekend.
*Sarah: Horseback?*
Susie: Yes, he got back about two hours before me!

**Knock Knock!**
*Who's there?*
**General Lee.**
*General Lee who?*
**Generally I go to training, but today I've got a match.**

**How do you stop squirrels from playing ball games in the garden?**
*Hide the ball, it drives them nuts.*

**What did one baseball say to the other?**
*"I'm outta here!"*

Millie went out for a ride on her pony. When she returned home, she was covered in mud.

"What happened?" asked Mum.

"Well," said Millie, "you know where the track forks after the village? Well, my pony wanted to go to the right and I wanted to go to the left."

"So what did you do," said Mum.

"We tossed for it and I lost!" said Millie.

Why don't grasshoppers go to football matches? *They prefer cricket matches!*

**Why did Cinderella get kicked off the baseball team?**
*She ran away from the ball.*

**What tea do footballers drink?**
*Penaltea!*

**What's a sailor's favourite snack?**
*Chocolate ship cookies.*

Which insect
doesn't play well
in goal?
*The fumble bee!*

Knock Knock!
*Who's there?*
Canoe.
*Canoe who?*
Canoe come out
and play today?

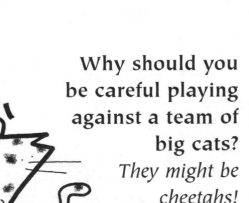

Why should you
be careful playing
against a team of
big cats?
*They might be
cheetahs!*

**What kind of leather makes the best hockey skates?**
*I don't know, but banana peel makes the best slippers!*

**What type of horses do monsters use for racing?**
*Nightmares.*

**Where does a sailor go when his sail gets a hole in it?**
*To the wholesale store.*

How do you stop
moles from digging
up playing fields?
*Hide their spades.*

What is Count Dracula's
favourite sport?
*Bat-minton!*

How can you swim
a mile in just a
few seconds?
*Go over a waterfall.*

# JUST HORSING AROUND

Three racehorses were standing in a stable bragging to each other one day. The first horse boasted, "I've run 59 races and I've won 35 of them."

"That's nothing," said the second horse. "I've raced 97 times, and I've won 78 of them!"

The third horse joined in, "Well, I've raced 122 times and I've won 102!"

Just then, the horses heard a voice say, "I've got you all beat!" The horses looked down and saw a greyhound. "I've raced over 200 times, and I've NEVER lost!"

The horses looked at the dog in amazement. Then one of them said, "How about that! A talking dog!"

**What did the tennis ball say when it got hit?**
*Who's making all that racquet?*

**What did the world's worst athlete do?**
*Ran a bath and came in second.*

**Why is a baseball stadium always cold?**
*Because it's full of fans!*

# LET'S HEAR IT FOR THE CENTIPEDE!

There was a big football game between the jungle animals and the minibeasts. The minibeasts were one player down. The jungle animals were winning easily. At half-time, the minibeasts' coach made a passionate speech to rally them.

At the start of the second half the jungle animals had the ball but the minibeasts soon starting getting the better of them. There was a penalty because the elephant was caught diving. Then the rhino got sent off for arguing with the referee. Then there was a free kick because the hippo was offside. At the end of full time the minibeasts were level with the jungle animals.

The coach rallied his players again before extra time. "Who made the elephant dive?" he asked.

"I did," said the centipede. "I tripped him up!"

"Who rattled the rhino?"

"Uh, that was me too," said the centipede. "I called him a 'snorter'."

"And how about the hippo? Who made him go offside?"

"Well, that was me too," said the centipede. "When I kicked the ball away."

"So where were you during the first half?" demanded the coach.

"Well," explained the centipede, "I was lacing up my boots!"

What's green, red and yellow and wears boxing gloves?
*Fruit punch!*

Why did the chicken get sent off?
*For persistent fowl play.*

What helps ghosts win games?
*Their team spirit!*

**What's a sailor's favourite food?**
*Naval oranges.*

**How long does it take to learn to ice skate?**
*A few sittings.*

**How does an octopus go onto the baseball field?**
*Well armed!*

# A YUCKY ICE FISHING STORY

Two men had been sitting out on a lake all day long ice fishing. One had been having no luck at all and the other had been pulling fish after fish out of his hole in the ice. The man having no luck finally leaned over and asked the other what his secret was.

"Mmmmm mmm mm mmmm mmm mmmm mmm."

"I'm sorry, what did you say?"

"Mmmmm mmm mm mmmm mmm mmm."

"I'm sorry, I still don't understand you."

The successful man spat something into his hand and said, "You've got to keep your worms warm."

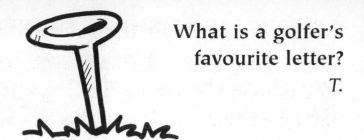

What is a golfer's favourite letter?

*T.*

What lives underwater and swims one hundred miles an hour?

*A moto pike.*

A coach was being interviewed after he had resigned from a football club.

"Weren't the crowd behind you?" asked the reporter.

"They were right behind me all right," said the manager, "but I managed to shake them off at the station!"

Sunil was sent home from school to collect his sports kit for games. When he got back he was soaking wet.

"What's happened to you?" asked his teacher.

"You told me I had to wear my sports kit for games," replied Sunil, "but it was in the wash!"

Why can't two elephants go swimming?
*Because they only have one pair of trunks!*

**What do you call a very intelligent tennis player?**
*A racquet scientist.*

**Why did the baseball smell?**
*Because it hit a foul ball!*

**What did the inflatable coach say to the inflatable rower caught holding a pin on the inflatable boat?**
*"You let me down, you let your team down, you let your school down, but most of all, you let yourself down."*

**Where do ghosts go swimming?**
*In the Dead Sea.*

**Why didn't the dog want to play tennis?**
*It was a boxer!*

**What do you call a girl who stands between the goalposts?**
*Annette.*

Sam said to his friend,
"I'm not going to play golf
with Jim anymore.
He cheats."

"Why do you say that?"
asked his friend.

"Well, he found his
lost ball two feet
from the green."

"That's possible."

"Not when I had it in
my pocket!"

Parent 1: What
position does your
child play in the
team?
Parent 2: *I think he's one
of the drawbacks!*

**Coach:** I'll give you fifty pounds a week to start with and one hundred pounds a week in a year's time.

*Young player: OK, I'll come back in a year's time!*

**When is a basketball player like a baby?**
*When he dribbles!*

**Why did the golfer wear two pairs of pants?**
*In case he got a hole in one.*

Why don't karate
experts salute?
*They might hurt
their heads!*

## A BONKERS BICYCLING STORY

By the time they reached the top of a
steep hill, two riders on a tandem bicycle
were panting and sweating profusely.

"Phew, that was a tough climb," said the
rider at the back.

"You're not kidding," replied the rider at
the front. "It was a
good thing I kept the
brakes on, or else
we would have
slid back down
the hill."

**What position did the two ducks play in the football team?**
*Right and left quack.*

**Harbour-master: There's no fishing allowed here.**
*Boy: I'm not fishing. I'm teaching my pet maggot to swim!*

**What did the left football boot say to the right football boot?**
*"Between us we should have a ball."*

# IQ TEST FOR FOOTBALLERS

1. What language is spoken in France?

2. Give a dissertation on the ancient Babylonian Empire with particular reference to architecture, literature, law and social conditions. Or give the first name of JAMES Bond.

3. Did William Shakespeare:
   (a) build a bridge
   (b) sail the ocean
   (c) lead an army
   (d) WRITE A PLAY

4. What time is it when the big hand is on the twelve and the little hand is on the one?

5. Spell — CAT, DOG, and PIG.

6. Six kings of England have been called George, the last one being George the Sixth. Name the previous five.

EXTRA CREDIT: Using your fingers, count from one to five.

# SILLY SPORTS BOOKS

How to Race Politely by Hugo First

The Winning Streak by I. M. A. Winner

Football Disasters by Owen Goal

Winter Sports for Softies by Kay Ping-Warm

Downhill Skiing by Bunny Slope

Guide to Fishing by Captain Hook

Anyone for Tennis? by Nettie Racquet

Who says I'm a Bad Loser? by I. Sulk

Snookered by Billy Ardball

Keep on Going by U. Ken Duitt

How to Improve Your Cricket Game by F. A. S. T. Bowler

Enjoy Swimming by Lee Do

Baseball Beginners by Fursten Base

Snorkling for Fun by Bubbles Galore

Exercise for Hamsters by Ona Wheel

Motor Racing for Beginners by Lerner Driver

**Pupil:** I've thought of a way to make the school team better?
*Teacher: Great! Are you leaving it?*

**What happened when Santa took boxing lessons?**
*He decked the halls!*

**Jane:** Did you hear the joke about the rope?
*Katie: No.*
**Jane:** Oh, skip it!

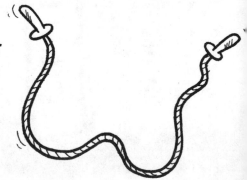

**Jack: You've got holes in your football shorts.**
*Ben: No I don't!*
**Jack: Then how do you get your legs in them?**

**What's the best day for sailing?**
*Winds-day!*

**Wanda's school team was trying to get into the top league.**

**"I'm sure we can do it," said Wanda. "We just need to win eight of our next four matches!"**

Why isn't it safe to make jokes when you're ice skating? *Because the ice might crack up!*

**What is usually found up a golfer's nose?**
*A bogey in the hole.*

**What do elephants play in a mini?**
*Squash.*

It had been raining heavily all week and the football ground resembled a swamp. However, the referee ruled that play was possible and tossed the coin to determine ends.

The visiting captain won the toss and after a moment's thought said, "We'll take the shallow end!"

**Where does Superman go bowling?**
*At Lois Lanes.*

**Why can't two waiters play tennis?**
*They only want to serve!*

Two lads were having their first cricket lesson.

"How do you hold the bat?" one asked.

"By the wings, of course," replied the other.

Class 5L were doing their exercises in the gym. "Next," said their teacher, "lie down on your back and bend and stretch your legs in the air as if you were riding a bicycle."

A few seconds later she asked, "Ginny, why aren't you pedalling?"

"I'm freewheeling, Miss."

**Why did Frankenstein give up boxing?** *He didn't want to spoil his lovely good looks!*

# A DIPPY DIVER

A diver was enjoying the underwater world. He saw someone at the same depth as he was, wearing no scuba gear whatsoever.

The diver went below another three metres or so, and the other person joined him a minute later. The diver went deeper still and shortly after, the same person joined him.

This confused the diver, so he took out a waterproof chalkboard and wrote, "How can you stay under this deep without any breathing equipment?"

The other person took the board and chalk and wrote, "I'm drowning, you moron!"

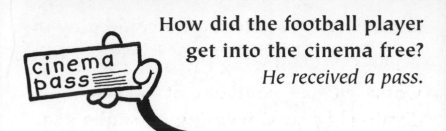

**How did the football player get into the cinema free?**
*He received a pass.*

**Why did the dinghy sailor always carry a bag of dried fruit with her?**
*So if she got into difficulty, the currants would carry her ashore.*

**Why was Bart Simpson kicked off the baseball team?**
*For hitting a Homer!*

**Frances:** The teacher said I could play in the school football team if it weren't for two things.

*Millie: What are they?*

**Frances:** My feet!

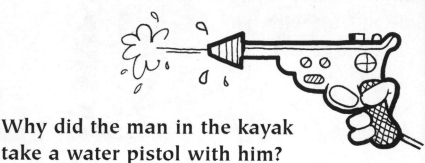

**Why did the man in the kayak take a water pistol with him?**

*So he could shoot the rapids!*

**What do sailors like in their soup?**

*Crew-tons.*

Two ice skaters were having a race.

As one passed the other she said, "Guess who's going to come first?"

"Not you," said the one she was passing, "because you're skating on thin ice!"

"Sorry I missed that goal," said Josh to his coach. "I could kick myself."

"Don't even try," said the coach, "you'd miss!"

**Alex:** My dog plays tennis.

*Tom: He must be very clever.*

**Alex:** He's not that clever – I nearly always win!

**Neighbour 1:** How do you like our new swimming pool?

*Neighbour 2: It's lovely, but why isn't there any water in it?*

**Neighbour 1:** We can't swim!

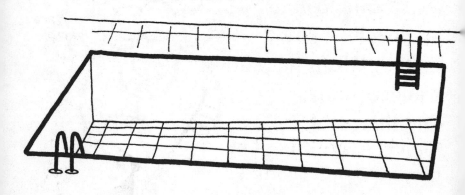

**What did the fisherman take home from the game?**
*The catch of the day.*

**How short can tennis shorts be?**
*They're always above two feet!*

**Coach: Our new midfielder cost ten million. I call him our wonder player.**
*Fan: Why's that?*
**Coach: Every time he plays I wonder why I bothered to buy him!**

Jo: I've got a real chance on the baseball team.
Chris: I didn't know they were raffling it.

What do you get if you cross a racing car with a computer?
Something that can crash at 200 miles an hour!

Why did the cricket team hire a cook?
They needed a good batter.

Rosie and Mike were having a great time in the snow.

"You can borrow my toboggan if you like," said Mike.

"Thanks," said Rosie. "Let's take it in turns."

"OK," said Mike, "I'll have it going downhill and you can have it going uphill!"

Why did Tarzan spend so much time on the golf course?
*He was perfecting his swing!*

**What's the hardest thing about learning to ride a horse?**
*The ground!*

**How do elephants dive into swimming pools?**
*Head first.*

**Why was the snowman hopeless at playing in big matches?**
*He always got cold feet.*

**What has twelve legs and two wings?**
*An ice hockey team.*

**Did you hear about the boy who tried to swim across the lake? When he was halfway to the other side he decided he was too tired, so he turned round and went back again!**

**What do athletes do when they're not running?**
*Surf the sprinternet!*

**Why is Dracula a hopeless goalkeeper?**
*Because he hates crosses.*

**Why did the high jumper check the calendar?**
*To see if it was a leap year.*

**Did you hear about the two men who ran in the fathers' race on sports day?**
*One ran in short bursts, the other in burst shorts!*

How many golfers does it take to change a light bulb?
*Fore!*

Did you hear about the boxing referee who used to work at a rocket-launching site?
*If a fighter was knocked down he'd count: Ten, nine, eight, seven . . .*

Fred turned up for the Olympics with some barbed wire under his arm. He came third in the fencing.

**Why did the runner bring his barber to the race?**
*He wanted to shave a few seconds off his time.*

**When is a swimming costume like a bell?**
*When you wring it out!*

**What do you call a boxer who gets beaten up in a fight?**
*A sore loser!*

A little girl watching a water-skier said to her father, "That man is so silly. He'll never catch that boat!"

What happens to a footballer when his eyesight starts to fail. *He becomes a referee!*

Why do elephants wear running shoes? *For running, of course.*

**What race is never run?**
*A swimming race.*

**Coach: Twenty teams in the league and you lot finish bottom!**
*Captain: Well, it could have been worse.*
**Coach: How?**
*Captain: There could have been more teams in the league!*

**My brother's a professional boxer.**
*Heavyweight?*
**No, featherweight. He tickles his opponents!**

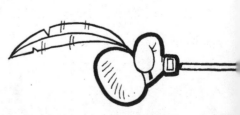

"I caught a twenty pound salmon last week."
*"Were there any witnesses?"*
"There sure were. If there hadn't been it would have been forty pounds."

What have a pool table and a coat got in common?
*They both have pockets!*

What has 22 legs and goes, "Crunch, crunch, crunch?"
*A football team eating crisps.*

After his horse lost the race, its owner was irate. "I thought I told you to make a rush at the end," he screamed at the jockey.

"I would have," answered the jockey, "but I didn't want to leave the horse behind."

What has eighteen legs and catches flies?
*A baseball team.*

What can you serve but not eat?
*A tennis ball!*

**What are Brazilian fans called?**
*Brazil nuts!*

**What kind of cats like to go bowling?**
*Alley cats.*

I wanted to have a career in sports but I had to give up the idea. I'm under six feet tall, so I couldn't play basketball. I'm only 190 pounds, so I couldn't play rugby, and I have 20/20 vision, so I couldn't be a referee.

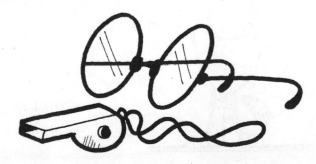

**What does the
winner of a
race lose?**
*His breath!*

**Knock Knock!**
*Who's there?*
**Willy.**
*Willy who?*
**Willy score?
Bet he won't!**

**Why are football
stadiums odd?**
*Because you can sit in
the stands but you can't
stand in the sits!*

# SEE YOU LATER, ALLIGATOR

While fishing off the Florida coast, a tourist capsized his boat. He could swim, but his fear of alligators kept him clinging to the overturned craft. Spotting an old beachcomber standing on the shore, the tourist shouted, "Are there any alligators around here?"

"Naw," the man hollered back, "they ain't been around for years!"

Feeling safe, the tourist started swimming leisurely towards the shore. About halfway there he asked the guy, "How'd you get rid of the alligators?"

"We didn't do nothin'," the beachcomber said. "The sharks got 'em."

**Why did the basketball player throw the basketball in the water?**
*Because his coach told him to sink it!*

**Why was the skeleton always left out in judo?**
*Because he had no body to go with.*

**What does it mean when you see eleven elephants wearing pink shirts?**
*They're all playing for the same team!*

# A GOOFY GOLF STORY

Once there was a golfer whose drive landed on an anthill. Rather than move the ball, he decided to hit it where it lay. He gave a mighty swing. Clouds of dirt and sand and ants exploded from the spot. Everything but the golf ball. It sat in the same spot.

So he lined up and tried another shot. Clouds of dirt and sand and ants went flying again. The golf ball didn't move.

Two ants survived. One dazed ant said to the other, "Whoa! What are we going to do?"

The other ant said, "I don't know about you, but I'm going to get on the ball!"

**Why did the football
quit the team?**
*It was tired of being
kicked around!*

**Knock Knock!**
*Who's there?*
**Caddy.**
*Caddy who?*
**Caddy your own
clubs, mate!**

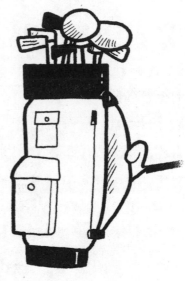

**Why is a tennis
game so loud?**
*Because the players
raise a racquet!*

**What's the quietest sport?**
*Bowling - you can hear a pin drop!*

**Why can't a bicycle stand up?**
*Because it's two-tyred.*

**Coach: I thought I told you to lose weight. What happened to your three week diet?**
*Player: I finished it in three days!*

**What is the best part of a boxer's joke?**
*The punch line!*

**Cloe: Were you any good at running at school, Dad?**
*Dad: Well, I once ran a mile in under four minutes. And if I ever find out who put those ants in my pants, I'll get him!*

**Mum: Did you get into another fight at the match today? You've lost your front teeth.**
*Son: No I haven't – they're in my pocket.*

**What did the bowling ball say to the bowling pins?**
*Don't stop me, I'm on a roll!*

**What is a goalkeeper's favourite snack?**
*Cheese on post.*

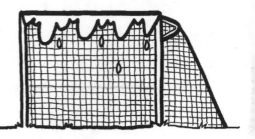

**How do hens encourage their sports teams?**
*They egg them on.*

Why can't bad
actors fish?
*Because they always
forget their lines.*

## WOULDN'T IT BE FUNNY IF . . .

**A tennis player needed a match?**
*A fighter needed a box for his ring?*
**A fisherman saw Annette?**
*A quarterback passed out?*
**A golfer joined a club?**
*A jockey felt hoarse?*
**A surfer waved?**